HOW TO START A CANDLE MAKING BUSINESS

A STEP-BY-STEP GUIDE TO MAKING AND SELLING CANDLES FOR PROFIT

By

Maxwell Rotheray

Copyright © Maxwell Rotheray – All rights reserved.

No part of this publication shall be reproduced, duplicated or transmitted in any way or by any means, digital or otherwise, including photocopying, scanning, uploading, recording and translating or by any information storage or retrieval system, without the written consent of the author.

Table of Contents

Introduction 7

CHAPTER ONE: How to prepare for success 11

CHAPTER TWO: Making the right connections 21

CHAPTER THREE: Candle making business checklist 29

CHAPTER FOUR: Raising Money for your Candle Making Business 37

CHAPTER FIVE: Cost of starting a candle making business 41

CHAPTER SIX: Finding the right location .. 45

CHAPTER SEVEN: Business Plan for Successful candle making business 55

CHAPTER EIGHT: Licensing your candle making business 65

CHAPTER NINE: Branding your candle making business 69

CHAPTER TEN: How to market your business for long-term success 77

CHAPTER ELEVEN: How to expand and establish your brand 87

CHAPTER TWELVE: Mistakes to avoid 91

CHAPTER THIRTEEN: Laws/Rules to abide by to avoid legal complications 99

Conclusion 107

Other Books by the Same Author 109

Introduction

Introduction

If you are passionate about starting a business and you are used to wicks, soy blends, probably with the full knowledge of a perfect scent, then going into a candle business may be a good fit for you. This book you are reading is a perfect guide on how to start a candle making business; keep reading because we are breaking down each step in the process.

If you finally decide to go into candle making business you will become a craftsperson as well as an entrepreneur. If that is the case, you are putting your creative talents and business acumen to good use as you are likely to cut a piece of the huge candle market. This book will give you an insight into the steps and resources you need to launch a candle making business.

Candle making business can be very demanding, but at the same time, can be very fun and rewarding. Before you allow your excitement push you into what you may not have the appropriate experience, pause and consider following this guide first. To hope of making headway in this business, you will need to put in place your financial, legal, technical and marketing ducks in a row.

To settle for a candle line, you can take a cue from these options:

- Candles specifically for churches with colours to match the liturgical church calendar

- Custom shape candles, for sports figures or animals

- Candles embedded with jewels or other kinds of treats.

- Candles crafted for unity, for use in wedding showpieces.

- Candles for "good wishes".

CHAPTER ONE: How to prepare for success

How to prepare for success

Having decided to go into candle making business, it is obvious you are going to take advantage of being;

- your boss

- able to do the work you enjoy doing

- able to invest and build upon something you enjoy.

- able to spend more time with family members

- able to determine your schedule of daily activities.

Besides, there are other reasons why a candle making business is a great business opportunity:

- The market demand for a candle is high: It has been established that in the US 7 out of 10 households use candles. People of all race use quality handmade candles and thereby supporting homemade products. Also, specially branded candles are in the range of most popular home décor items found in the market.

- Relative ease to start: The candle business doesn't require a lot of capital and equipment to start, indeed you just need basic supplies, tools and a workspace to get the business off the ground. To master the business is a matter of a few weeks.

- Marketing candle product is simple: The market for the product is readymade and what you are required to do is to make quality candle products. There are outlets to promote candle sales such as the farmer's markets, gifts shops, craft malls and online--both your site and others such as Etsy.

- You're never on your own: Once you have become a candle making entrepreneur, you have automatically become partakers within the candle making communities where knowledge and other resources are easily shared.

Planning for Success

No matter the scale of your operation, creating a business plan is crucial in determining what the roadmap is likely to be. It gives you an indication of what the future of your candle making business will be like, layout the basis for your brand, and set up the framework for success.

So to be able to achieve success in this candle making venture, it is imperative to develop a framework to guide you in reaching your goal. The following steps should get you close to achieving a good measure of success.

Develop your brand proposition

What brand of candles are you going to make? To answer this question calls for research to determine the most economically viable and strategic brand of candles to concentrate on.

You could use one or two sentences to describe the core values of your candle business and the value of what you want to deliver to your prospective customers.

Define your target market

Your candle brand cannot be everything to all people or attempt to serve every candle user; you must define your market from the customer's point of view. So decide to build your brand around the following broader candle market.

- Mass-market: This is the market for the masses and typically many retail stores are outlets where these candles are sold. They are the less expensive candles you find in the market; made with economical containers and packaging materials.

- Mid-market: You can also make candles targeted at the broad market such as Macy and Target, or the local boutiques and other gift shops. The price range of these candles should be between $9 and $14

- High-end market: Candles found in this market command a premium price and they are usually prestige-level products that you can buy from stores like Nordstrom, Saks Fifth Avenue and other upscale boutiques. The price range is from $15 to $25

However, before going into production, it is important to identify which market to serve, what are the market characteristics, the basic reasons for their purchase and how much they are willing to pay. This information is crucial in determining the materials to use in the candle making and at what market level you are going to place your brand of candle.

Find your unique selling proposition

You should identify what makes your product (candle) unique and stand out from competitors. The following are some of the common ways some marketers of candle find their niche:

- Unique scent combinations
- Very attractive packaging
- Funny names
- Support for a good charitable cause

On the whole, you will aim to market candles that are unique and are special to your genre; which is very difficult to find elsewhere.

Craft a unique brand name

Choose an individual and corporate brand name for your product and business. Craft a logo, colour scheme and something that identifies your brand. You will need to create a website and make sure the chosen name is available. You may need to register a trademark, but it might not be necessary at this stage but you can keep the option open until when such a time as the business gains momentum.

When you are working on the possible names for your business, concentrate on what makes your brand unique, the values you are passionate about, and what you think will attract customers to your brand.

Build a startup budget

Budget is essential particularly for a new business because it provides estimates of the initial cost of starting the business. With the budget of the first three months, you will be able to have an idea about the cost of supplies, equipment, and other indirect expenses.

Come up with an initial product line

It is essential at this stage to keep the initial product line low so that you will be able to manage it. Determine the fast-moving products in the market and if they match your target market, go for it in the hope that you will add more lines in the future. You will also find out the cost of production and the appropriate price to charge your customers. You will be advised to take a holistic view in determining the selling price such as what competitors charge, cost of production, the demand for the candle and what customers can afford.

Locate your market.

Initially, begin to promote your brand around your friends, family and other business and social networks; they can provide invaluable feedback on your candles and as time goes on can be your brand ambassadors

The market for your candles is not hard to find, there are three markets you can concentrate upfront and expand to other markets when appropriate. These markets include the following:

- Farmers markets, local gift stores and craft shows

- Online marketplaces

- Your website including the use of Shopify to market your candles

Register, procure insurance and obtain permits and licenses

It is a legal requirement to incorporate your business, procure liability insurance, and obtain permits and licenses. However, it depends on your location and possibly your business needs. Therefore, you must consult your attorney, accountant and insurance broker for professional advice.

Besides, you also need to explore state and local permits and license needs for small businesses. There is also the need to determine whether to register your business name, register a partnership or incorporate an LLC; each has its advantages and disadvantages, and it depends on your business needs too. Your attorney and accountant will certainly be of help here.

CHAPTER TWO: Making the right connections

Making the right connections

Establishing good connections can be profitable in the candle making business and it can be achieved by getting involved in community projects and even beyond. Candle making business is the type that needs knowing so many people if you want to succeed. You have to befriend people who work for the local boutique who sell scented and premium candles to people who buy from high street stores. You will create opportunities for doing things together with great folks who do great things in your community. It is also a wonderful idea connecting with industry competitors, knowing the big players and what makes them tick. But first and foremost, find out what it takes to associate with your local people and contribute to the community to get you noticed and recognized.

- **Promote your local community unique cause:**

You can begin by finding out what makes your community different from others, the values and philosophy under which they were built

You can search for the values and ideologies your community is made of and what makes them what they are. Look for it and promote it. Incorporate it into your business as if it is part of your business and have the sticker on your signage. Naturally, your local community will be excited to see it. Find out other things that make your community proud that you can promote; they may include the following:

- Your City's celebrated anniversary or founder's day and get it to implant on your merchandise.

- Celebrate with your local sport's heroes when they win tournaments.

- Create a radio jingle, a slogan, or make a logo that is a symbol of local pride.

- Name some of your candle lines after local champions, memorial sites, and landmarks.

- **Endorse and promote other people**

You will probably get noticed when you promote others pursuing a charitable cause. Sharpen your eyes, you will notice special events happening in your local community, you will find out that some notable people or organizations are sponsoring it. These are local businessmen and women like you and they are sponsoring charitable cause and other great people taking up great challenges to raise funds for a good cause. Be ready to promote those people; you will rest assured that it will go a long way to connect you to your community.

The following are some of the smart ways to promote other people and businesses in your area:

- Share human interest stories from local news outlets about inspirational people and businesses.
- Use your Facebook page and Twitter to share some people and businesses especially in the candle making industry that enjoy a tremendous measure of popularity in your neighbourhood, and pass on good wishes to them

- **Head-Up a Cause**

If following others doesn't inspire you, you can come up with your own cause for the benefit of your community. It could be a campaign against women oppression, military rule, extrajudicial killings, or lack of government support in your area. Your cause is an indication of support for your community and your contribution to its cause, and the people will be happy to see you as fighting for their cause and this will go a long way to get you and your business connected to your people.

If you are financially able, you can also help in promoting any of the following causes:

Victims of a natural disaster within your area.

Motherless home in your community

Victims of the COVID 19 lockdown particularly students who can benefit from online coaching

- Donate for a just cause

If you are unable to organize something on your own, then look out for someone else in your area doing a similar thing, you can lend your moral support as well as making financial donations, or your time, as the case may be.

You can also find out in your area whether there are charitable organizations in dire need of a financial assistant, donate generously but remember to get such donations publicized.

- **Sponsor physically challenged peoples' sporting event**

Supporting sporting activities organized for physically challenged people is another way to get involved in community affairs. This option makes you known all the way through but more importantly, it makes you an integral part of the community.

- **Local Advertising**

If you are looking for cheap publicity, and indeed getting your brand name and logo recognized within your neighbourhood, instead of donating to kids' sporting events, you can choose to advertise your brand of candle business in the local newspaper and radio. You can also have your posters signage around the town particularly at crossroads and within highly populated areas.

- **Participate in Events**

Participating in events that take place in and around your community particularly exhibitions and trade-fairs. You should also attend other events such as concerts, sports or anniversaries because it is a means of making friends and building relationships. If you drive, get your car painted with your business colour and logo, and if possible park at a place your car will be conspicuous.

If there is an opportunity for a candle or candle related show, please do attend because it is an occasion to socialize with other candle makers and captains of the big retail outlets. Be ready to share pleasantries with the people and make valid enquiries to learn more about the candle business. Always have a budget for a charitable cause so that you don't deeply upset your business budget.

CHAPTER THREE: Candle making business checklist

Candle making business checklist

The following is the candle making kit checklist you need to get started in the candle making business.

1. Wax

Wax is very essential in candle production and it is what keeps the wick burning and melting and then vaporize. But wax is of different types and they serve different purposes. Different types of wax include:

Beeswax

- Beeswax is an expensive type of wax that has a sweet scent. It is harvested from beehives, burns slowly because of its higher melting point.

Paraffin wax

- Paraffin wax is a flexible type of wax used for everything from moulded to poured candles.

Soy wax

- Soy wax makes good sense because of its natural oils and also it mixes well when joined with other fragrances. Meanwhile, the burning is clean and when compared with other compounds, it is found to be cheaper.

Tallow

- Tallow which is made from animal fats tends to produce smoke and a pleasant odor while burning. The good side of it is that it is colourless as well as a low melting point.

Bayberry wax

- Bayberry wax produces a sweet floral scent with a low melting point. As a result, it costs higher than most waxes.

Gel wax

- Gel wax doesn't have natural oils; it is odorless but has a high melting point. Gel wax is better for candles that are themed but the downside is that it doesn't mix with additives smoothly.

2. Wick

Wicks release fuel it draws from the candle to the flame. Their performance is largely affected by the quantity of fragrance added to it; the dye, and the type of wax in use.

In candle making, the following are the common kinds of wicks in use:

Flat wicks

- These types of wicks are made of three consistent-burning braided fibres. These fibres are self-trimming and are mostly used for pillar and taper candles.

Square wicks

- These types of wicks are immune to wick clogging and mix better with scented additives. The square wicks tend to be ticker than the flat wicks, this creates the flexibility of usage and the great absorbance quality.

Wax coated wicks

- The wick that has been pre-dipped in wax is wax coated wicks. They are great with smaller jar candles and headlights but are not suitable for candle gets

3. Molds or Containers

Often, molds or containers are made with three different materials: metal, plastics and silicone.

Plastic and silicone molds deliver diverse sizes and shapes more, making it great for delivering remarkable and cool candle shapes while metal will produce the best finish.

4. Double Boiler

A double boiler or a bain-marie, is recommended in the melting of candle wax since it doesn't burn the wax. Though it may sound complex, the vast majority of people already have the tools they need to assemble one.

5. Heat Source

Also, you'll need a heat source such as a hot plate or a stove to melt your candle wax.

6. Fragrance Oil

Fragrance oils are important additives to any type of candle because they give the candles a soothing aroma of food, spices, flowers, and other relaxing scents.

7. Candle Dye or Color

If you want to color your candles, you'll also need candle dye. A variety of dye is easily available and it can be purchased online. They are also available in different varieties such as liquid, block, and flake.

8. Other Sundry Supplies

These fall under a whole range of items that include measurement, utility, and decoration.

A scale is needed for measuring your wax, fragrance oils, and dye. A thermometer is also required for making sure the melted wax is kept at the right temperatures.

You will also need a set of hot glue gun and sticks when positioning the candle wick on the bottom of your chosen container. Similarly, the following are also needed to keep your work surface, hands, and skin protected from hot, melted wax or glue.

Labels and other decorative items are also essential for giving your DIY candles their own unique aesthetic and feel. They're great especially if you're planning on using these candles as gifts, as the decorations can adapt to the occasion.

CHAPTER FOUR: Raising Money for your Candle Making Business

Raising Money for your Candle Making Business

The common methods of raising money for your candle making business are as follows;

1. Bootstrapping

Funding your candle making business may not be compulsory. Many entrepreneurs use this approach to start their business irrespective of the fact that they have a substantial amount of money to get started.

So, what do you understand by the word, Bootstrapping?

Well, it simply means to self-fund a business without having to raise capital or looking for external help and reinvesting your profits back into the business. Some tips you need to consider when bootstrapping your candle making business are as follows;

- Start a business that will bring quick profits to reinvest back to the business

- Instead of hiring, consider outsourcing.
- Be lean as possible – try to cut down expenses like avoiding unnecessary travel, fancy software, payroll, renting an office, etc.
- Use your savings as your capital – the perfect method to bootstrap your candle making business is to use your savings as startup capital. This will avoid you from using your business or personal credit cards when getting started.
- Before you get your business off the ground, determine how much capital you need and how much capital you have.

2. **VC Funding**

Although this may be a traditional and long process, it is also an effective method to raise money for your candle making business.

VC represents venture capital which indicates investing in businesses in exchange for equity.

The perfect approach for businesses with high startup costs is the VC's. Nevertheless, it is crucial to keep these few things in mind when deciding on whether to adopt this approach;

- Determine if your business is ready
- Get everything in place and build a pitch deck
- Research the right VC to fund your business
- Ensure the expectations and terms are right for your business.

CHAPTER FIVE: Cost of starting a candle making business

Cost of starting a candle making business

Depending on local zoning laws, you will probably be able to start your business anywhere including right inside your home kitchen, using your heat source and utensils. A starters' kit of products can be purchased from many online stores. You will need to purchase the following for your candle making business:

- Wicks
- Paraffin, gel, soy, beeswax or other wax
- Essential oils for fragrance
- Packaging supplies
- Jars, tins or other containers (but you don't need containers if you are solely marketing pillar candles)
- Coloring agents
- Packaging supplies

- Shipping costs of raw materials in and finished candles out

You will need to pay for other start-up costs such as web development, and at least a reasonably good camera. If you plan to promote your products at trade shows and festivals, a booth is also essential, and can cost about $100 a day; you'll have to pay for gasoline and related travel costs. The cost of the above materials cannot be determined accurately without market research or window shopping, and therefore attaching prices to them will be misleading.

Re-current expenses for a candle making business

The candle business utilizes essentially various forms of wax, containers, color and fragrance additives. Once you've set up your business on a small scale, and your model begins to work, you can buy the above items in large quantity at reduced prices. For instance, the wax is sold as little as a dollar a pound when bought in 25-lb quantities. Wicks can be purchased by the 100-ft. spool. Containers, including glass jars, mason jars and tins, may also be purchased in bulk quantities.

CHAPTER SIX: Finding the right location

Finding the right location

It is not difficult to discover marketplaces to sell your candles. You can sell your candles in these three markets;

- Gift shops, festivals, local craft shows, and farmers market
- Online marketplaces such as Etsy
- Your website (it is recommended you use Shopify since it is a great resource).

You might have had thoughts on where or even how to start selling candles, but with these three sales channels listed above; it can be tough to know where to begin. The three sales channels come with their benefits and possible or likely challenges.

Besides, a lot of businesses that are successful start with just one sales channel before switching to a multi-channel approach to improve their profitability.

1. **Selling Locally**

Are you the type that knows how to communicate and convince people to buy your products? That said, personal rapport is known to be the huge advantage of selling in local stores rather than selling online. You have the opportunity of communicating with your customers and also let them take a look at the product, touch it, and even perceive your product (candles) before buying the product. In most cases, there are very good options of selling your candles in local stores.

The few places you can consider to sell your candles include;

- **Farmers markets**

A casual way to step into the world of local selling is the farmers market. If you have no idea about the farmer's markets, simply visit the National Farmers market directory or go to selling at farmers' markets from Shopify to get more information.

- **Craft Fairs and festivals**

Craft fairs and festivals which is a bit similar to farmers markets let you to make direct sales and get valuable feedback. Go to Festival Net CrafterLister to search for nearby events. You can also visit your local chamber of ecommerce websites. Also, a good social media platform that can offer a great resource for local craft fairs is Facebook.

According to an expert, otherwise known as D'Shawn R., Southern of Elegance Candle Company, selling locally allows you to know if your branding is cohesive enough. You can introduce your brand to people, get a customer base, and hear all types of feedback. He added that all of these options are so invaluable.

Also, according to another expert, otherwise known as Heather B., selling locally gave me the confidence to grow my business. At first, I was shy and nervous, but I eventually got overwhelmed with all the support from strangers praising my products. It encouraged me to attend larger shows, meet local shop owners, and start wholesaling my products.

2. **Online marketplaces such as Etsy**

There are also some huge advantages to selling online. Some of these huge advantages include flexibility, good geographic reach, and low startup costs. According to research, a growing number of people prefer to shop online since it is convenient enough. And since there are various new platforms and tools available, selling online either on social media platforms or websites are stress-free than ever to launch and manage.

Some of the options you need to explore if you desire to sell online include;

- **ETSY**

Since Etsy is regarded as one of the top marketplaces for creative entrepreneurs, customers can easily access your candles posted online. What you are only expected to do is to post your candles for a price of $0.20 and a 3.5% commission.

If you must know, people who use Etsy to sell their products reach out to over 26 million active buyers. And since the candle business is very popular, you can decide to sell your products through this platform.

- **Social Media**

Another online platform you need to consider in selling your candles is the social media platforms. They can be of great assistance especially in terms of marketing your business, although you can use the social media platform to directly sell your candles to your customers. The two primary options to sell your candles include Facebook and Pinterest.

3. **Your website (it is recommended you use Shopify since it is a great resource).**

It might sound scary or even frightening when you want to create a website but it is not. Once you own a website, you have full control over it and the rate of making a profit is increased. Even if you are not exceptionally good with online activities, you can easily design a site with less cost using any of these platforms;

- Squarespace: Entrepreneurs who intend to emphasize beautiful aesthetics and photos should consider this platform.
- Shopify: This platform should allow you to create a custom online store, process shipping, take credit card orders, add social media platforms, and also mix plug-ins to develop your candle business. A very good bonus of using this platform is that it offers lots of learning tools.

Wholesaling candles

What do you understand by the word, wholesaling? Well, it is when a person sells a particular product such as candles to retailers for resale at a markup. You can expand your streams of income and suitably sell in volume to a single client, have access to the existing customer base, and receive positive feedback on what sells best.

If you want to successfully wholesale products, then you need to take shelf-ready products and also a professional brand such as candles. These following options can help you wholesale candles to retailers;

- Shops: a very good introduction to the world of wholesaling is the local shops. Try to know the owners of stores and share your products and brand. Since a lot of candle businesses target shops in other states, do not try to limit yourself to local stores.
- Boutiques: Another fantabulous method of wholesaling your candles is the boutiques. Boutiques are a better fit for a high-end target market.
- Etsy Wholesale: Do you own an Etsy shop? If you do not, you can simply

apply to Etsy wholesale and access more than 25,000 stores. But before you can be qualified, you must have a constant record as an Etsy seller and own a professional brand. To check if you are eager, simply have a look at Etsy's wholesale guide, glossary, or worksheet.

CHAPTER SEVEN: Business Plan for Successful candle making business

Business Plan for Successful candle making business

What does it feel like when you are earning profit selling a particular product or brand? To cut the long story short, we will be giving a detailed explanation on how you can start a candle making business with little amount of capital.

You as an entrepreneur can earn additional income for exploring a small scale candle manufacturing business. If you want your candle making business to be successful, then you need to consider the following options;

Can you make a profit in selling Candles?

In 2018, the global candle market accounted for 8.4 million dollars. Experts of the industry also anticipate that it would grow to 13 million dollars in a few years.

If you have a good marketing strategy and also plan properly, then you can earn a lot of profit from the business. Do not be bothered about the cost of making candles because it is very low. The profit margin is much better than many other consumer products. A person who sells candles can easily earn a profit percentage of more than thirty per cent.

It will take at least 12 weeks to achieve the break-even and the expected gross profit which could rise to 40 per cent.

Plan Guide for Candle Making Business

We have a list of how every entrepreneur should commence a profitable candle making business either at home or on small scale.

You can initiate a candle making business with a small start budget from home. You are wrong if you feel people only purchase candles for religious activities. A lot of people purchase candles to decorate their homes or business places.

- **Learn the steps of making candles**

First and foremost, you learn the basic steps of making candles. If you want to make a perfect candle, then visit an online class, experts, or even the National candle Association's website @ www.candles.org.

Make sure that the candle burns from start to finish with a strong and pleasant scent. Besides, make sure that the candles burn evenly with no residue left on either side of the jar.

- **Permits/Licenses needed for candle making business**

If you are about to commence a candle making business, you should have with you the legitimate business documentation irrespective of the location of the business. Discuss with your lawyers and accountants to acquire the knowledge of what permits you need to take while commencing and operating a candle making business.

- **Select a Business structure**

Select a business structure that appears proper because you might use it to run your candle making business. Distinctive states offer varied alternatives for forming a company. Let us take for instance; if you reside in London, forming a sole proprietorship will not cost you much; although LLC will offer you certain benefits with additional cost.

Open a business bank account after receiving the necessary documents. Discuss with any insurance company and select the appropriate one you want to buy.

- **Select what products you intend on selling**

Similar to other kinds of businesses, once you find and concentrate on a specific niche; you should experience success in your candle making business. If you are yet to know, a candle is a product that can be used for numerous purposes and kinds by its nature.

Before you start a candle making business, try to do some market research. If you want to start a white color candle business, you need to determine the shape and size. If you want to start a scented candle, you need to determine the kinds of designs, colors, and shapes you will be making.

You will also have to decide on the kind of candle you intend selling, that is, votive, soy, tea light, hurricane, gel, wickless, pillar, scented, novelty, or jar candles.

- **Write a business plan for your candle making business**

Every successful candle business has a written business plan which comes with details of information about the niche and target audience. The written business plan also has information about marketing the products and public relations plans.

When you want to write your business plan, make sure you include three-years expense budget with profit projections and a detailed analysis of competing for candle segments.

Let us assume you want to start your candle business on a small scale or even at home, you are only required to explore some basic aspects such as; target market, choosing the right name for your candle making business, startup and recurring costs, financial analysis, that is, when your business is going to reach the break-even stage.

- **Create the ideal setup**

If you want to make and ship the candles, simply set up a work area; although you need a computer for managing orders. Besides, you are expected to create a logo and print materials such as business cards, letterhead, catalog, and brochure of your business.

Also, make sure that every candle you intend selling has an appropriate warning label or write an instruction on how each candle should be properly handled or used. If your candle making business is low-cost or even home-based, then it needs time management, discipline, and organizational skills. Make sure the price of your candles is fixed and competitive to guarantee a profit.

- **Raw Materials for candle making business**

Go in search of vendors of reliable raw materials. Note that these raw materials include fragrance, wax, crafts, and color supplies. Fragrance trends are crucial since it is usually seasonal.

Consumers demand more for candles which comes with added fragrance and color. Besides, you should focus on other ornamentation associated items such as jars, brawls, etc.

Some of the basic items you are required to procure for making candles are as follows;

1. Wicks
2. Colouring agents
3. Fragrance oils
4. Packaging supplies
5. Paraffin, soy, gel, beeswax, or some other wax

6. Tins, jars, and other containers according to the items you intend to make.

- **Look for places to sell your candles**

If you want to introduce your candle items, simply contact nearby retailers and wholesalers. Gift stores, craft fairs, home stores, and grocery stores are possible customers of candles.

Also, create an online store if you want to sell online. An online store will help in showcasing your items. Some other market places you can showcase your candles are Etsy, Amazon, eBay, etc. You only have to register yourself as a seller and sell your candles.

- **Bookkeeping**

If you are just starting a candle making business, you need to note the process of recording all financial transactions on a day-to-day basis. Recording all financial transactions will help in analyzing the financial health of your business. Besides, if you are serious about the business, then you can consider the accounting software.

- **Promotion of candle making business**

If you want to start selling candles, you can rent a table at a craft store in a nearby place. Besides, you can sell candles by placing the candles in a retail location with a consignment agreement.

To get a big audience for decorative scented candles, simply sell them at restaurants, spas, or hotels. If you want to be professional and knowledgeable, simply market yourself more than your business product. Make sure all products are checked before you place them in the market. Also, create a website for your business and register your business with B2B portals to get online leads.

CHAPTER EIGHT: Licensing your candle making business

Licensing your candle making business

The license and permits needed for any candle making business include the following;

- Company registration: First and foremost, initiate your candle making business by registering it in the form of an artificial legal business entity such as partnership, sole proprietorship, limited liability, or even company.
- GST registration: As long as your candle making business is under GST, your business is mandated to carry out a taxable supply of goods or services. And if your business turnover or sales goes beyond the threshold limit, then you have to register and obtain a GST number.
- PF registration: It is obligatory upon the unit management to acquire or register under EPF since there are

more than 20 employees in a manufacturing unit or company.
- ESI registration: Especially in India, it is mandatory for all businesses to acquire an employee's state insurance (ESI); but only if the business employs 10 or more employees.
- Pollution Certificate: As long as an establishment commences its activity, it must have already obtained a No objection certificate from the state pollution control board.
- SSI Registration: it is entirely at the discretion of the application to either register it as SSI unit or not. The SSI registration is not compulsory.
- Trademark Registration: Every successful candle making business maintains the uniqueness of its product by acquiring a trademark for its product. This trademark will prevent the business from harming the market by competitors or save him from being concerned about duplicating the product.

- Insurance: It is also compulsory for not only a candle making business but other businesses to get it inured to mitigate the liabilities and risks.
- Business License: Every successful candle making business operates in their various cities by acquiring or obtaining a permit from the concern local department.

CHAPTER NINE: Branding your candle making business

Branding your candle making business

As long as it concerns branding your candles, it is recommended to start with a logo and design. Branding your candle collection has more to it than just the pretty labels and beautiful scents. Every entrepreneur that sells candles will have to consider everything that goes into selling it which includes packaging, containers, and marketing materials.

Each step in a consumer's candle buying process is a step to build your brand. From purchasing and accessing the candle to launching and burning it, there are several branding flashes you can take advantage of.

Irrespective of the fact that you intend to hire a graphic designer or create your unique artwork to brand your candle collection, accomplishing a cohesive look across the whole line of marketing materials and products is crucial.

Do not be bothered about branding your candle collection because we have put together some different ideas using tags, labels, and card products to explain how you can easily carry your brand across other materials.

Labelling your candles

The most important aspect of branding your candle collection is the label. While the end-user observes that the candle is burning, he also notices the label.

Let us assume your brand is the star of the show, it would be wise of you to select special shaped or large labels. Selecting a clean jar with a vivid label is important especially if you desire the beautiful colors of your candle wax to shine through.

If you also want the look and feel of your candles to be exceptional, simply add additional coordinating colors to the marketing materials and exterior packaging.

Do not end at the candle jar

Irrespective of the fact that your candles might be shipped to individual customers from your online store or the candles are purchased in a boutique or shop, it is recommended to add a hang tag or even an extra label to the outer packaging to make it more appealing.

If you want your customers to experience a ready-made gift, simply add a custom tag to the box it is packaged or to the candle itself. It is not necessary to wrap the candles. Besides, the brand of your candle collection can be extended if you follow these procedures.

Also, it is perfect to add hang tags because it creates an extra fun touch to bags, candle jars, and boxes. If you want to tie directly around your candle container, simply use a piece of colored twine. You can also include tags to carry-out bags for retail locations.

Another special method of branding and sealing your candle boxes at the exact time is by using the large rectangle labels. If you manage to place the candle inside the box, just add a custom to wrap around the label.

Never stop networking

It is a must to have professional business cards on hand that complement your brand irrespective of the fact that you make huge sales.

You can be conversing with a nearby passenger in a restaurant or on a bus about your product. And you might expect, it could eventually result in a sale.

It might be easy to add your contact or number to their smartphones, but it could also be lost if it is not saved. Printed business cards that appear pretty usually arrive at an individual home. But if you want your cards to have more interest, simply add a special offer on the back of the business card.

Always promote

Now that you must have labelled your candles, tied up your packaging, and also printed out your business cards; simply continue to promote your product and never stop. Since there are available online design tools, it is easy to create personal coordinating marketing material. Let us assume you are making use of the design tool from Avery, you can continue with the same design on your business cards, labels, and tag, to ensure your brand is consistent across your whole candle line.

Loyal customers are simply your perfect tool for bringing in new business through referrals. Another exceptional method to offer sales through direct mail or as handouts at the farmer's market or street fairs is by coordinating postcards. By enclosing personalized cards in completed orders, you should be able to treat loyal customers to special discounts.

Easy methods of creating your marketing materials and candle labels

Assuming you are fully prepared to begin branding, labelling, and packaging, simply visit a Candle design gallery site. In there, you will learn a variety of free templates and easy-to-customize templates. What you should do is to select your favorite design and personalize it for your whole candle line.

Also, select the perfect shape and size you desire, then personalize and either have them professionally printed by Avery or print them yourself using Avery blank labels by the sheet.

CHAPTER TEN: How to market your business for long-term success

How to market your business for long-term success

You might be making sales on scented candles or other kinds of candles, but what you should keep in mind is that knowing who it is that you are selling to is important to the success of your business.

When you are visualizing your buyer's persona, simply consider these three primary factors;

- Spending Behavior:

    Do your customers always buy premium-grade candles? Do your customers shop online? Do your customers love deals? What are the similar products these customers usually buy? If you know these behaviors, then you should be able to align your marketing in the right area. When you want to create your buyer persona, ensure to include these details.

- Demographics:

    Geography, age, gender, and more are significant because it will help create better targeting methods for your promotions. You should begin by creating a buyer persona or a fictional customer that has a higher chance of purchasing your candle.

- Attention:

    What consumes the attention of your customers? You need to identify some important aspects to guide your marketing placements. Let us take for instance; creating Facebook ads for your customers may be a very good option since most of your customers spend time on social media sites.

Know the perfect sales scents and seasons for your candle business

You can go miles in your candle making business if you have a good grasp on your calendar. There are numerous periods around a calendar year for candle sales to skyrocket and it is certainly crucial to know the period of purchasing a few extra pounds of wax.

Below, we have some good examples of seasonal scents;

Season   Example scents

1. Summer   Sea salt, beach, wine, citrus, coconut, sandalwood, peach, citronella,

   Hay, Aloe, linens, grass, watermelon

2. Spring   Cherry blossom, apple blossom, lemongrass, jasmine, lavender,

   lilac, magnolias, lilies, honeysuckle

3. Winter   Cinnamon, cookie, peppermint, vanilla, maple, nutmeg, orchid,

juniper, pine, chestnut, birch

4. Fall   Amber, Pumpkin spice, sage, apple, eucalyptus, cedar, brown, cinnamon, brown sugar tobacco

As long as you showcase this sort of resourcefulness and flexibility with scents in your candle business, you will definitely instill confidence in your customers by proving to them that you are there for them throughout the year.

Make sales of candles in the slow seasons

You should not feel down because you are experiencing slow months. This is not the period to reduce the pace of your marketing efforts. You should rather concentrate on the products that sell throughout the year and also promote them for numerous uses.

Some of the marketing ideas for seasons that are slow are as follows;

- Allow customers to access small gifts on their birthdays
- Give a discount to your email list
- Create fun promotions by using incomprehensible holidays as a humorous excuse.
- Promote gift ideas for graduates or even teachers.
- During the slow seasons period, try to maintain your social media posting to keep everyone' much loved or preferred candle 'top of mind.'

Promote your business online

Since 2019, online sales became the most crucial place for marketing. As long as you remember your value propositions, seasonal relevance, and buyer personas, simply follow these tactical candle marketing ideas to promote your business;

- Choose your social media channels: Since candles are usually attractive or charming, ensure to select the perfect visual platforms for these products. Pictures are a big pull on platforms such as Facebook, Instagram, and Twitter; so it is vital to invest in these three platforms.
- Create a content calendar: If you want to keep your audience engaged, simply plan out your post ideas. Customers would always want to look forward to your post as long as you post enough; although you should not post too much. You should maintain a healthy frequency if you create and stick to a calendar.
- Brainstorm Themes and ideas: Keeping in mind your brand, simply create ideas that align and have emotional impacts on your audience.
- Design and write: Your posts should also be designed and they should always come with a caption.

Use Online Ads to reach New candle users

Online platforms flourish on selling ad space. Simply go to Google and Facebook to sign up. If you want to gain the best clicks directly to your website, simply use any of these platforms (Facebook and Google).

Explore Extra initiatives to marketing your candle business

- Blogs: If you want your candle making business to be recognized, then you consider having a blog.
- Forums: Similar to blogs, forums are a platform where you can commune with your customers who show care about your industry and brand. The only difference is that you will also discover other business owners who carve up techniques and useful opinions involved with their business.

Ensure Repeat customers with Email Marketing

A massive indicator of favor with your brand is by subscribing to newsletters. You will certainly be accumulating email addresses from your customer irrespective of the fact that it is voluntary from your website or automatic from purchases. Begin a monthly newsletter by sending one every month. Send the same one on two occasions each month if it is successful. Platforms such as Mailchimp ensure that every designed and sent email is top-notch.

Ensure Customers are engaged with your business

It is very easy to engage your customers in an online space. It takes only seconds to comment and post which will certainly bring in hundreds of dollars in the long-run. More work is required if you are engaging directly to a person. Some suggestions are as follows;

- Host candle-making classes in your space
- Sell at markets and local events

- Invest in ads and printed flyers in your community.

CHAPTER ELEVEN: How to expand and establish your brand

How to expand and establish your brand

First and foremost, custom labels can assist you to expand and establish your brand if you are starting your candle making business. These custom labels present a personalized and special look if you are making it for favors or gifts.

That said, you will want to add some other information on the label. Some of this information includes the following;

- Any warning or caution messages
- The kind of wax
- Event name or business name
- The weight of the candle
- The scents of the candle
- Photo or logo

You will always have a professional presentation for your candles when you are done with the following.

TIP: If you want your logo or image file to print clearly, then you must allow it to be

300 pixels per inch in resolution. You can consider using a fascinating font to highlight the name of your business if you do not have a graphic or logo of any kind.

Also, irrespective of the fact that you pour your candle wax into candle tins, candle molds, or glass jars, your candle-making expertise will be enhanced with the right label. You will have to use one of the longer water bottle label sizes to wrap a label around your candle.

Brand Candle Boxes

As long as you add a custom label to the inner box, you are directly extending your branding. Select from squares, rectangles, circles, hang tags, or ovals.

Selecting a Label Size

The most crucial thing you need to do when you want to determine the size candle container (tin or glass) is to measure the area where the label fits. To determine the maximum width or height of the label area, simply use a flexible measuring tape. After that, you can know the perfect label size on your container. If you are sceptical about this, just get a piece of paper and cut it out in that size. Then, hold that same paper against your container.

Some of the sticker sizes you can consider when selecting a label include;

- 3 inches square
- 3 inches wide by 1.5 inches high
- 2 or 2 ½ inch circle
- 3 inches by 2 inches in landscape or portrait orientation
- 2.25 inches x 3.5 inches oval in landscape or portrait orientation
- 8 inches wide by 1.75 inches high to wrap around large pillar candles
- 3 inches by 4 inches in landscape or portrait orientation

CHAPTER TWELVE: Mistakes to avoid

Mistakes to avoid

Starting a candle making business can be exciting and even fun. It is also another method of utilizing some creativity. Nevertheless, there are various things you need to consider before starting your business. In another meaning, simply avoid mistakes that can make your candle making business to go under before it even gets started.

- Avoid beginning the business with no experience

Just like any home business, you cannot start without having at least some experience. In essence, before you start a candle making business, you must have made candles or even soaps probably as a personal gift, etc.

More time will be required and also the risks will be higher if you start any kind of business with no experience.

If you must know, you should have some background, to begin with, if you can manage to take a class at a local community center or even having a look at a candle making book.

- Avoid not making research or having any business plan

Any business must have a plan that goes hand-in-hand with a lot of research. You are currently at the base start if you are only making candles for fun or as a hobby. If you want to be professional or business-minded, then it needs some planning.

Your research must focus on where to get bulk supplies such as the candle base (soy, beeswax, gel, or paraffin), molds, dyes, scented oils, or wicks.

Besides, you will also have to select a business name along with registering your business with your Local County or city. Even if you might not consider this option, you may also need a business license especially if your candle making business is from home. Most businesses in different locations have their business license.

- Avoid having no workspace

If you have decided on starting your business from home, then you need to ensure that the space needed for the business is available and appropriate to accommodate your candle making business. Candle making business requires a much-needed space for different activities such as a place where you can melt your candle material, etc. Also, you need a specific area where you can store your molds, candle making essentials, melting pot, oils, and wicks.

- Avoid having no niche

As long as you want a business that is related to candle making, you must decide on a specific niche. Let us assume you enjoy making a specific kind of candle and are efficient in making these types of candles, you should entirely focus on it. Let us take for example, assuming you are so good or you probably enjoy making soy candles, you should simply stick to it until you are prepared and eager to expand and establish your candle making business.

- Avoid having no market

It is also crucial to choose how and where you will sell your candle immediately your business becomes official. The perfect way to market your products (candles) is to have a website; although there are many other ways.

Irrespective of the way you sell your candles, you must ensure that the price of the product is right so that you keep gaining customers and maintain a customer base. As you know, it will certainly result to profit for your business.

In conclusion, once you can avoid these kinds of mistakes in your candle making business, you should experience fun and make the maximum profit in the long-run.

- Avoid when the candle emits smoke after it gets burnt

Some of the likely causes for this kind of experience would be;

1. Air pockets in the candle
2. A high essential oil content or fragrance
3. Over-wicking

Avoiding such mistakes only requires you to;

1. Reduce the amount of essential oil content or fragrance. It is recommended to add between 10 to 12 per cent of the total weight of wax.
2. You can warm up the container for ceramics or glasses
3. It is normal that the larger the number, the larger the wick if it is within a series of the wick. Nonetheless, burning the candle can be affected by the different waxes, colourants used, and the essential oils or fragrance.
- Avoid Holes, cracks, and air pockets in the candle

If water gets in contact with your container or mould, then your candle may experience holes, cracks, or air pockets. Another likely cause is the temperature of the wax which is normally poured into your container or mould. You can experience air pockets in your candle if the temperature of the wax is lower than its recommendations.

That said, to avoid such mistake, simply warm up your container or reheat your wax.

- Protect the candle from wicking drowns out

This often occurs when;

1. When the wick you initially cut is too close to the wax
2. When the wick is much lesser in size for your candle diameter
3. When your container changes shape as a result of the candle you poured.

You can avoid or even fix such mistakes by;

- Changing to a larger wick

- Making sure that the candle does not affect the container shape
- Having at least 1 centimetre between the wax and the tip of the wick.

CHAPTER THIRTEEN:
Laws/Rules to abide by to avoid legal complications

Laws/Rules to abide by to avoid legal complications

As long as you use a candle safely, it will always give many hours of atmosphere and beauty. You should also experience a great sensory if the candles show their sophisticated fragrances and elegant colors. Even though candles are mostly used as decoration, it does not change the fact that they are burning with an exposed flame. In other words, these works of art which may appear lovely can also pose a potential threat to human health.

The National Candle Association (NCA) which is located in the United States has played a major role in the creation of a set of candle industry standards. The ASTM international on the other hand has helped to develop and publish these standards.

These standards vividly outline crucial attributes that need to be adhered to. Besides, these standards are intended to assist combat the increase in the number of fires as a result of the candles.

When you head over to the candle subcommittee page of the ASTM information, you will have access to the six vital standards along with the full information and detailed description. Let us break it down; the six standards are as follows;

- "Standard Specification for Fire Safety for Candle Accessories
- Standard Guide for Terminology Relating to Candles and Associated Accessory items
- Standard specification for Fire safety for candles
- Standard Specification for candle fire safety labelling
- Standard Test method for collection and analysis of visible emissions from candles as they burn
- Standard Specification for Annealed Soda-Lime-Silicate Glass containers that are manufactured for use as candle containers."

Trading Standards

Once you begin selling candles, your leading body will automatically be the local authority Trading Standards. Let us assume you are not sure or even confused about anything, it would be worth your while to have contact information for them to hand or directly contact them.

The applied law to you and your candle making business is the General product safety regulations (GPSR 2005). It may not be designed for the sale and production of candles or may not even have any specific laws to follow, but it contains the European standards which must be complied with when selling candles. You will display a lack of due attentiveness or thoroughness if you fail to do so.

Online selling

Similar to what other candle businesses do, you will be making sales on your product across different channels, from online stores to social media accounts. There are some things you need to keep in mind especially when doing so. If you sell this way, then it means you will enter a distance contract with your customers. And it simply indicates that you give your customers two weeks right to cancel and supply pre-contract information.

Let us assume you own a social media account or even a business website, the following business details must be provided;

- Legal ownership name
- Business name
- Email address
- Geographical address (the location you can deliver legal documents)
- VAT number but only if you are registered

The customers or consumers need to know the legal requirement of your business since they are entering a contract. This also applies to physical sales and these rules and regulations are covered under the Companies Act 2006 and e-commerce Regulations. The details of your business should be present on invoices, receipts, and business correspondences like emails.

Business Insurance

If you want to safeguard yourself against any unforeseen circumstances, then ensure your business has insurance. Numerous insurance companies will provide craft insurance that covers this type of business (candle making). It is advisable to shop around to locate the perfect cover at the perfect price. Even though the labelling on your product is correct, the consumer might still charge you to court and you might face large legal bills. Thus, safeguard yourself and your business.

Extra Label information

Most successful businesses ensure that the label is correct. This correct label consists of all applicable CLP documentation for each candle.

Let us assume you are selling a product that has a similar appearance to other products or has similar scents, you should keep in mind the extra-label recommendations. In other words, every candle product that a kid may think it is a food product that can eventually lead to injury or death should be prohibited. This applies to small products such as wax melt that appears so much like cakes and sweets.

Nonetheless, you as a supplier should not be bothered about things you must do to avoid this outcome because once you mark out your packaging like 'Do not Eat', 'Not Food', then it will certainly help. The other crucial things you can investigate is how to make your product more child friendly and also how you package your product.

Assuming your product is registered with The Health and Safety Executive' (HSE), then you are allowed to sell and label a candle as an insect repellent. You can also sell and label a candle as an insect repellent if you have scientific information backing this up. Due to false advertisements or even misleading statements, you could land yourself in trouble if you fail to have any of these mentioned above.

It also applies to making other claims like the burn time and fragrance efficiency. The only way you can make these claims is when the provisions you have can back up your statement.

The Consumer Protection from unfair trading regulations 2008 cover misleading actions, professional diligence, and misleading omissions associated with any business adverts, marketing materials, verbal descriptions, and labels descriptions.

Conclusion

The main theme of this Book is to show how anyone can succeed in candle making business. As long as you take the right steps and market the right products, thereby making a profit, you should be able to establish your foothold in the marketplace in the shortest time possible and also expand your business.

All the same, you must be mindful of the fact that this type of business (candle making business) which is similar to other types of businesses comes with its special challenges and risks. Some of the risks and challenges are common to many businesses and proper handling of business asset and management of liability is required to ensure business success and continuity. Therefore, the profit of your candle making business is usually determined by your ability to manage your business and avoid risks that can put your business in jeopardy.

Other Books by the Same Author

- How to Start a Photography Business: A Beginner's Guide to A Successful Career as A Photographer
- How to Invest in Real Estate (For Beginners): Make Your First $100,000 Using This Powerful Real Estate Business Model
- How to Start A Drop Shipping Business: Make Your First $1,000 Using This Powerful Drop Shipping Business Model
- How to Start a Cleaning Business: Make Your First $100,000 Using This Powerful Commercial Cleaning Business Model
- How to Start a Life Coaching Business: Foolproof Guide for

Establishing a Successful Life-Coaching Career

www.ingramcontent.com/pod-product-compliance
Lightning Source LLC
Chambersburg PA
CBHW031435210526
45464CB00005B/2208